Pack it!

Claire Wood

Illustrated by Christine Cuddihy

Schofield & Sims

Ram can pa<u>ck</u> a top.

Eta can pack a top.

Ram can p<u>ck</u> a so<u>ck</u>.

Eta can p<u>ck</u> a so<u>ck</u>.

Ram can pa<u>ck</u> a cap.

Eta can pa<u>ck</u> a cap.

Ram and Eta in the sun!